I0164323

Disciplines
of
Joy

McDougal & Associates

Servants of Christ and Stewards of the
Mysteries of God

Disciplines
of
Joy

by

Rachel Elizabeth Gregory

Disciplines of Joy

Unless otherwise noted, all scripture quotations are from the *Holy
Bible, New King James Version*, copyright © 1979, 1980, 1982 by
Thomas Nelson, Inc. Nashville, Tennessee. References marked
KJV are from the *Holy Bible, King James Version*. References
marked NLT are from the *Holy Bible, New Living Translation*,
copyright ©1996, 2004, 2007, by Tyndale House Foundation,
Carol Stream, Illinois. References marked NIV are from the
Holy Bible, New International Version, copyright © 1973,
1978, 1984 by International Bible Society, Colorado Springs,
Colorado.

Published by:

McDougal & Associates
18896 Greenwell Springs Road
Greenwell Springs, LA 70739
www.ThePublishedWord.com

McDougal & Associates is dedicated to the spreading of
the Gospel of Jesus Christ to as many people as possible
in the shortest time possible.

ISBN 978-1-940461-10-6

Printed on demand in the US, the UK and Australia
For Worldwide Distribution

Contents

How I Came to Write This Book

In the summer of 2009, I had a dream. In that dream I was given a book. The book cost something. It cost time and effort.

The title of the book was *Disciplines of Joy*. Over time I received many chapters. Then one day I knew that the summer of 2013 would be the time to write this book.

I am grateful to all those who have contributed to my life and those who have given me words of encouragement.

Introduction

Joy is not merely an emotion. Joy is a choice. It is a choice to believe God and all His promises. It is a choice to enjoy every good and perfect gift. It is a choice to lovingly look into the Bridegroom's eyes across the table, even in the presence of your enemies. It is a choice to love the One who loves you.

In the fullness of His presence, you'll find joy, you'll find rest.

Rachel Elizabeth Gregory
Concord, North Carolina

And these things we write to you

that your joy may be full.
1 John 1:4

Chapter
1

Worship God

You shall love the Lord your God with all your heart, with all your soul, and with all your mind. [1]

Worshiping God is the most important thing that you can do. It is paramount. Worship God every day. Let your prayer and praise come before the

---

1. Matthew 22:37, NIV

Lord of Hosts. He is the King of Glory. In His presence is joy forevermore. At His right hand are pleasures eternal. He loves you with all His heart. Love Him back.

We do love Him because He first loved us. He is so wonderful. Focus on His goodness. Focus on His love, His joy, His peace. Focus on His faithfulness, His lovingkindness, His patience. Focus on His gentleness, His self-control. He is the best God and Father you could ever hope to have.

When times are hard and you can't see the way, worship God. Get your focus off the problem and back onto a good and gracious God. Let your love and affection be for Him alone. Don't let your focus be on the circumstances or anything else. God loves you, and He will make a way for you. He is the best God ever.

God is always good. Trust in Him to do everything for you. Let Him be your trusted Friend forever. Love the Lord your God with all your heart, mind, soul, and strength. He will do for you all that is for your good. He is the Lord.

God is always there for you. He will never leave you or forsake you. He understands all your hurt and pain. He understands all the hard things no one else can. Worship God because He is God. No one else is in control of anything in the Universe. He alone is God, and He loves you and cares for you.

God is always good. He will never be vindictive. He will see you through. Don't wait until things change to worship Him. Worship Him now. Give Him the gift of your love and affection. Give Him the gift of your time and your praise.

Worship God when things are good. There is nothing good apart from Him. He is the Giver of every good and perfect gift. God alone is good. Enjoy the goodness of His presence. Love Him with all your heart.

Worship Him in song and dance. Worship Him with your uplifted hands. Worship the Lord in your thoughts. Rest in His goodness and in His faithfulness. Find your own way of expressing your love to Him.

Worship the Lord. Daily spend time in His presence. Look for new ways to give Him glory. Enjoy your relationship with your heavenly Father.

Time spent with the Lord will change you. You can know His transforming love and joy. You can know His peace. You will know the truth, and through that truth, He will set you free. He will set you free from every bondage and every oppression. He will lift every load. Break the yoke of the enemy from your life.

You can cast all your cares upon the Lord because He cares for you. He will sustain you.

You don't have to worry. You can be assured that He loves you. You can trust Him. He will make a way for you to be joyful in every trying situation. Your trials are brief. Your afflictions are momentary. And through them God is working for you a far more exceeding and eternal weight of glory.

Let the love of God flood your soul. Your faith will be increased. The fiery darts of the enemy will be extinguished. You can continue confidently ahead because Jesus has gone before you. You can trust Him to provide for you all that you need.

Jesus is Lord. He is the Healer of every emotional pain. He is the Provider of all your needs. He will give you joy for your strength. You will make it. He will bring you through.

Let God change you through worship today and let Him receive all the glory.

Chapter

2

Take Your Thoughts Captive

We take captive every thought to make it obedient to Christ. [2]

It is important for your thoughts to be captive and obedient to the Lord Jesus Christ. You can choose to con-

---

2. 2 Corinthians 10:5, NIV

trol your thoughts or you can let your thoughts control you. Choose to think positively. Think on whatever is good, pure, and lovely. Think on the things that are of good report. Think on that which is praiseworthy. Think on the things that cause you to give glory to the Lord. Think on that for which you are thankful.

As a man thinks in his heart, so is he. Do you want to be joyful? Then think on joyful things. Transform your thinking by the reading the Word of God. Know His truth. Spend your time in prayer, not in vain imaginations. Get God's viewpoint on your situation. Know that He has chosen you for a purpose. Isaiah 43:18 tells us that He has chosen us to proclaim His praise.

Reject all negative thinking. Let there be no worry, no criticism, no complaints. When we observe the example of the Israelites, we begin to see the awful results of negative thinking. Worrying about giants, doubting God's ability to deliver them, and not believing that He was able to defeat their enemies caused them to literally refuse to enter the abundant blessings of God.

Being critical was also a disaster for them. In Numbers 16, we read that the earth opened up and swallowed three rebellious leaders with all that pertained to them. Fire also came down from Heaven and consumed two hundred and fifty men in that same rebellion. Still not having learned this important lesson, the next day all the congregation of Israel again complained. This let loose a plague that killed 14,700 people. Ironically, the leaders who made atonement for the Israelites and stopped the plague were the very ones the others had complained against.

Don't let worry lead you to evil. Don't judge another man's servant, examine yourself. And don't let the destroyer into your life by complaining. Repent quickly. Encourage right thinking in your life. Sinful thoughts are just that — sin. Don't let sin rob you of your God-given joy.

Don't get trapped in endless mazes of *"what ifs."* Don't waste your mental energies on imaginary conversations. Don't imagine every possible outcome of what you will say or what you will do, or what you should have said or done. Say *no* to every vain imagination. Our God is in control. Let the Lord turn the mind of the king whithersoever He wills. Let Him handle the outcome. Moment by moment, be led of His Holy Spirit.

If you really need to talk about the situation, then go for a walk or sit down and tell it all to Jesus. Yes, He knows it all already, but tell Him anyway. Tell Him every trial, every struggle, all the anguish. Tell Him all the truth. Then when you are through, leave it with Him. Don't continue to struggle trying to figure it all out. Let Him be God because He is God. Rely completely on Him. Give Him control. Yield your life to His will. He has promised to work all things together for your good. You don't have to understand how. Simply trust Him. He will direct your paths.

Chapter

3

"Remember Not the Former Things"

Remember ye not the former things, neither consider the things of old. Behold, I will do a new thing; now it shall spring forth; shall ye not know it? I will even make a way in the wilderness, and rivers in the desert ... to give drink to my chosen, my people ... . They shall show forth my praise.[3]

3. Isaiah 43:18-21, KJV

God wants you to be prepared to move forward with Him. Don't be so caught up reliving the past that you miss out on the good things that He is doing now. Refuse to be weighed down by the past. Lighten your load, so that you are ready to move when He is. Do not let the past hold you back. You have a future with God, and He is waiting to meet you there. Even one day of bitterness is too much. Give these things over to the Lord. Get ready to move!

Let the past be past. Look forward in Jesus. He is the Alpha and Omega. He is the Beginning and the End. He is the Author and the Finisher of your faith.

God has plans for you. Plans for something good, something refreshing, something new. You belong to Him. You are His child. You are chosen by the Lord. What has He chosen you for? He has chosen you to proclaim His praise.

Look forward to what the Lord has for you in the here and now. Make a conscious effort to live in the present. God's plans for you are for your good. Don't let the enemy rob you of all the good that God has for you in this time. Lighten your load. Let go of the past. Put it under the blood of Jesus.

No one can change what has happened, but you can change. You can be who God wants you to be. You can be anything God says you can be. You can do anything He says you can do. You do have a future with God.

You have a lot to look forward to in the Lord. You have a heavenly home. You have an eternal inheritance. You are being conformed to His image. He will cause you to triumph. Don't give up.

Do not let yourself get trapped in the old way of thinking. Let your mind be transformed by the Word of God. Be renewed in the spirit of your mind.

Drink deeply of God's fresh, new, and living water. Don't try to quench your thirst with the old, stale, stagnant water of the past, and do not stay in the old place when God has moved into something new. Get where God wants you to be. Live in His times.

Plead the blood of Jesus over your past. Resist any spirit that would bring the former things to mind. Ask the Lord to wash you and cleanse away old memories. Live in the now with the great "I Am."

Let God's new thing spring forth in you. He has many wonderful plans for you. Don't hold on to the past. Let go and receive God's best. Get ready to move!

Chapter
4

Let Other People Receive Their Own Answers from God

To be obedient, one must be submissive.
It doesn't mean being a doormat or not
having a mind of your own.
It means preferring to do God's will,
even when you want to do something
else.

God doesn't want robots or cookie-cut-ter Christians.
He wants genuine individuals whose goal is to please God. [4]

Pray for others, but then let them receive their own answers from the Lord. Don't you try to solve their problems. God's ideas are much better than your ideas. His ways are higher than your ways. His thoughts are higher than your thoughts.

When you let other people get their own answers from God, you let Him be their guide through all of life's mazes. Remember that He is their heavenly Father, too. A father's answer is always better than any brotherly or sisterly advice. Let God lovingly guide them in the way He sees is best. His way is best for them and for all concerned. God is

4. Poem 19 by Ann Pope, used with permission

infinite and His answers are infinite. There is no limiting the blessing of the Lord. His way is best for all.

Remember that God loves them more than you do. He gave His all for them. Jesus suffered, bled, and died for them. Jesus ever lives to make intercession for them. You may truly care, and you may really love them, but human love has limits. God's love is eternal and all-powerful. There is nothing good for them that the He will withhold from them.

Maybe you do have a good idea for someone else. Wait on the Lord. You may be amazed to see that the idea you thought originated with you is being put into place, implemented, without a word from you. Then, when it is not working out quite the way you thought, hold your peace. Be amazed the second time to see the other person change things around, again, without a word from you.

When Jesus was confronted with the woman caught in adultery (in John 8:3-11), He not only loved the woman; He even loved her accusers. When they asked Him what should be done to her, He was silent a long time and kept writing on the ground. When He did give His answer, it was *"He that is without sin among you, let him first cast a stone at her"* (John 8:7, KJV). This was an opportunity for her accusers to search their own hearts and look to God. The Lord obviously gave each man the answer that he, too, was a sinner in need of salvation.

Jesus did not accuse them or tell them to leave her alone. He let each one receive his answer directly from the Father. And each one did silently admit his own sin and left the woman in peace. Let us trust the Lord to have His way without our help.

Instead of offering advice, offer up prayer and praise to the Lord for the individuals you care about. Then let God speak His Word directly to them. How wonderful! God speaking directly to His children, showing His love and concern with a specific word of direction for their lives! Just think how they will feel when they know God cares enough to communicate directly to them. And He knows just the word to speak to them, the word that will open up their hearts to receive all of God best.

Don't get in between a loving heavenly Father and His child. Let others have full access to their Father. He sees the things you don't see. He knows the best solution. He won't give them more than they are able to handle. If they ask for bread, He won't give them a stone. If they ask for a fish, He won't give them a serpent. If they ask, He will give them the Holy Spirit. Our Father in Heaven is perfectly capable of raising His own children. Your job is to simply be who God has called you to be.

Love others. They are not the problem. Love them with the love that God provides. His love is shed abroad in our hearts by the Holy Spirit, which He has given unto us. His perfect love casts out all fear. Fear of your loved ones making mistakes has to go under the authority of the Holy Spirit. Fear of the outcome or fear of the future? It, too, has to leave under His authority. God is in control. He is in control of our lives, and He is in control of theirs.

God will supply the answer, so begin praising Him now for all He is doing behind the scenes that you know nothing about. Praise Him for deliverance from every besetting sin. Praise Him for that person's salvation. Begin praising Him now, for His answer will be so glorious that you will be praising Him through all eternity. Get started now.

Our God inhabits the praises of His people. Invite the Lord into the situation with your praise. Praise Him in everything. Thank Him that He is in control. Thank Him that His throne is established in Heaven. Thank Him that His Kingdom rules over all. You are not without God. You are not without hope. You have God on your side and on the side of your loved ones, as well.

Do not forget to wait patiently for His answer. You will have need of endurance, so that having done the will of God you may inherit the promise. While you are waiting, keep thanking Him for His good and perfect will. And when He gives you a little glimpse of the promise to come, write it down and keep it. Whenever God gives you a promise, hold on to it tightly. Do not forget it. Every day that seems to pass without the answer is actually one day closer to the fulfillment of God's Word. If He gives you specific directions to follow, then follow them. If it's hard and you don't think you can do it, pray and ask God to be at work in you, both to will and to do of His good pleasure. Expect Him to handle the outcome. Expect a miracle.

Chapter
5

Believe God

To fully lean on God,
To know that He is in control.
We have to exercise our faith to trust Him.
Flesh wants to worry and fret, but we have to stand on faith.

Uncertainty of this life,
Testing of our faith,

Coming to the place of faith,
Realizing that God is in control,
Holding on to the faithfulness of God [5]

Faith is also a discipline of joy. First, choose to believe that God is. Believe that God loves you. Believe that He is in control. He is working all things together for your good, and the good of your loved ones as well.

Faith is the substance of things hoped for, the evidence of things not seen. By it the elders obtained a good report. I want to have evidence of the things I am hoping for in God. I want a good report. I want to hear how God has wrought a mighty work.

When things do not seem to be going well, choose to believe God. Believe He will take care of the situation in the best way for all concerned. Seek God's direc-

---

5. Poem 23 by Ann Pope, used with permission

tion. Let Him tell you what steps to take and when to take them. Trust Him with the results. They will be God's business.

Obey as fully and completely as you can. When you have difficulty, ask God to help you have both the desire and the ability to do His will. He will help you. You are believing God when you choose to follow His way.

When you have chosen to believe that God is in control, you can relax. He will bring about the victory. You don't have to worry or try to figure out a plan. He has a plan already, a plan for your good and His glory. You can now offer up prayer and praise and thanksgiving for all He is doing — known and unknown. You can praise God that He is abundantly able. There is nothing impossible with Him.

If you lack faith, ask God. He will help your unbelief. Faith is also a gift. Faith is a gift that your heavenly Father is longing to impart to you. You have not because you ask not.

Faith is the evidence of things not seen. Faith helps you joyfully and patiently wait for the manifestation of the answer from the Lord. Until it does manifest, you have your faith as the evidence that it will surely come. You are now encouraged and strengthened. You will make it through to your expected end, your promise from God.

You only need a little faith to please God and accomplish great things. Faith as tiny as a mustard seed can move mountains. Remember Elijah at Mt. Carmel (in 1 Kings 18:16-39). Elijah's set-up for fire, soaking wet and surrounded by water, was not a picture to promote success. Surely any spark of fire would soon be quenched. But fire did come down from Heaven and consume the sacrifice. Remember that God is able to do exceeding, abundantly above all you ask or think.

Even if you forgot to ask, He is still able. You might not have asked for a miracle, but God can still supply one. If you never even thought of this possibility, He has it covered. Our God is all-powerful and all-knowing. There is none like Him. He is the Alpha and the Omega, the Beginning and the End, the Great "I Am." Our God is amazing, and His love and care never cease to amaze us. There is faith for you, your shield from God.

Chapter
6

Do Not Agree with the Words of the Enemy

But the people held their peace and answered him not a word; for the king's commandment was, "Do not answer him." [6]

When God commands you to be silent, hold your peace. Be quiet. And

_____

6. 2 Kings 18:36

be at peace. Rest in the Lord's unfailing goodness. Trust in Him also, and He shall bring it to pass. Do not agree with the words of the enemy. The Lord is able to save to the uttermost.

Do not agree with the enemy's opinion. Do not even repeat it. A lie seems to carry greater weight each time it is repeated. It will definitely weigh you down. And didn't you just pray to lay aside every weight and to run with patience the race the Lord has laid out for you?

Get in agreement with the Lord and His words. If life and death are in the power of the tongue, then speak life. Be in agreement with the Lord Almighty. I am sure He is right. All His words are true. All His promises are sure. You can count on the Lord. He is a can-do God.

Get in agreement with the Holy Spirit here on earth. Jesus said that if any two of you agree on earth concerning anything, it shall be done for them. So, who better to be in agreement with? Be sensitive to the Holy Spirit's leading, especially in your prayers.

Encourage yourself by speaking out the Word of God. Remember the things that are eternally true, and let them come forth from your mouth. You might not be able to see it, but the sun is always shining. You just need break through to see it. How things seem may not be how they are. What darker time than the crucifixion of Christ? The sun literally did not shine in the middle of the day. Yet God was working out His eternal plan of salvation. He saw the Son rising on the third day. He saw Him bringing many sons to glory. Jesus' focus was on the joy set before Him.

Begin now to receive by faith the reality of God. Do not let others deceive you. Know the truth of God's Word for yourself. Repeat your God-given promises out loud. Reinforce the truth of God's Word. Let it go out of your mouth, into your ears, and return to rest in your heart.

Resist every feeling of oppression. You have the victory. Give glory to God. Let the meditations of your heart and the words of your mouth be pleasing in His sight. He is your Lord and your Redeemer. Stand firm in the absolute and eternal truths. Jesus is Lord. If God is for us, who can stand against us? If He did not spare His own Son, how will He not freely give us all good things?

Do not argue with the enemy. Do not agree with the enemy. Do not repeat the enemy's words to others. Do not let his words ring in your ears or go through your mind. The Lord is able to save to the uttermost.

Simply lay the situation out before God (see 2 Kings 19:14-37). Don't rehash it. Just say, "Lord, there it is." God is God and He alone. He commands and none can reverse it. When you pray to God about a situation, He hears. He will defend you from the enemy of our souls. God can do the impossible. He will save you and your loved ones.

The story of King Hezekiah and his battle against the enemy is told in 2 Chronicles 32. He said, *"With us is the* L*ORD* *our God, to help us and to fight our battles,"* [7] and *"Be strong and courageous; do not be afraid nor dismayed."* [8] God is with you, not just to help you, but also to fight your battles for you. In this instance, King Hezekiah did absolutely nothing but keep quiet and lay the situation before the Lord. It was the Lord who sent out an angel that killed 185,000

7. 2 Chronicles 32:8
8. 2 Chronicles 32:7

of the enemy forces — every leader, every captain, and every mighty man of valor. There was none left to fight. The enemy king went shamefacedly home, to be killed by the very ones he had trusted. With you is the Lord your God to help you and to fight your battles for you. With the enemy is only an arm of flesh. Nothing can withstand the Lord.

"Rise up Army of God. The Son is shining over you. There is power in Jesus' name. You are an army of God. No chains are holding you back. Wake up! There is a call on you. There is a call for you. Don't let the enemy lie to you, [saying], 'You have this issue. You have this issue in your family.' " [9]

---

9. A prophetic word spoken by Brenda Naska, missionary to Philippines, at Evangel Worship Center, Concord, North Carolina, in 2013

In Jesus' name, dark powers are broken.
In Jesus' name, we'll be set free.
In Jesus' name, a great revival will come into this land.
In Jesus' name, there's victory.

In Jesus' name, blind eyes are opened.
In Jesus' name, we all can see.
In Jesus' name, a great revival will come into this land.
In Jesus' name, there is Victory. [10]

---

10. Chorus by the author

Chapter
7

Look to the Lord, Not at the Problem

"Keep your focus on the Lord. He'll send help. Let God do it His way. He can send you the help you need." [11]

There will always be plenty of bad things to think about. Focus on the Lord. [12]

11. Pastor Thant McManus, Evangel Worship Center, Concord, North Carolina
12. Ibid

It is true. There will always be plenty of bad things to think about, but you keep your attention on the Lord. You do not want to miss what He is about to do. It will be wonderful.

Challenges will come. Don't meditate on them. And don't keep agonizing over your situations. Focus on the Lord. *"Life is a journey, not a destination."*[13] Your promise is in Jesus. All the promises of God for you in Christ Jesus are in Him "yes" and "amen." Are you in Christ? Have you asked Jesus to be both your Lord and Savior? If so, then He is the one responsible for you. Start obtaining your promises. Don't miss out. Look in the Bible to see what promises are there for you. They are your God-given gifts.

Meditate on the Lord. Think on how wonderful He is. Focusing on the prob-

13. A quote from Ralph Waldo Emerson I found on a necklace purchased at the Rowan Cabarrus Community College Bookstore in Salisbury, North Carolina.

lem is looking through the wrong end of the telescope. The more you focus on the problem, the bigger the problem seems to get. Each retelling of your woes seems to set them in cement. Let it go. Focus on the Lord. Whatever He is up to is wonderful. Get excited about what God is doing, whether or not you know what it is. Be confident in who God is, not in who you are. God is more than sufficient. The Lord is bigger than any problem. He is stronger.

God is wiser. He is completely worthy of your trust. Focus on Him and see reality. All your afflictions are light and momentary in the light of eternity with the Lord.

Give your situation over to the Lord. Pray about everything, and then let Him handle it. Take the steps He orders you to take, as He directs you to take them, but do not worry about the outcome. And do not worry about what the next step will be. He'll give you the direction you need when you need it. Wait on the Lord. He will send the help you need. He sent the Holy Spirit to be our Comforter and our Guide. He is the one who empowers you to be His witness. He will empower you to do all the things He commands. The Lord will give you the strength to overcome. He will give you the clarity to focus on Him. He will give you love and faith to forgive. Pray about everything. Then let Him take over. Thank Him that He is still God, and He is in control.

When we see Jesus, we will be like Him, for we shall see Him as He is (see 1 John 3:2). By faith, look to the Lord. If you can't do anything else, simply raise your eyes to Heaven and cry out to the Lord. He is your Helper, your Redeemer, your Savior, your Deliverer, your Friend. He is not just your Savior; He is the Savior of all mankind. Receive all that God has for you, not just what you think you need. Receive His love, joy, peace, patience, kindness, gentleness, goodness, faithfulness, and self-control. Don't miss out on God's best.

Every slip-up is another chance to choose God's way of thinking. If you catch yourself focusing back on the problem, make the conscious choice to think on the Lord. Get His viewpoint. He is never running around trying to figure out what to do next. He is seated in Heaven. His throne is established in Heaven. His Kingdom rules over all.

Think about a few of God's rules. He will finish the good work He has begun in you. All things will work together for your good. You are being conformed to His image. Relax and be assured: God has it all under control.

Chapter
8

Be Thankful

In every thing give thanks: for this is the will of God in Christ Jesus concerning you. [14]

By prayer and supplication, with thanksgiving, let your requests be made known to God; and the peace of God, which surpasses all understanding, will

14. 1 Thessalonians 5:18, KJV

guard your hearts and minds through Christ Jesus. [15]

Nor [let us] complain, as some of them also complained, and were destroyed by the destroyer. [16]
He who promised is faithful. [17]

You have two choices in every trying situation: you can be thankful or you can complain. You can choose to be thankful and come into God's presence. You can know His joy and peace. Or you can choose to complain and let the enemy into your life to destroy you. Will you open the door for the Lord Jesus Christ? Or will you open the door to the enemy of your soul? The thief comes not, but for to steal, and to kill, and to destroy. Whom

15. Philippians 4:6-7
16. 1 Corinthians 10:10
17. Hebrews 10:23

do you want to invite into your situation? To whom do you want to yield?

Be thankful. Don't be destroyed by the destroyer. You are commanded to give thanks in everything, not in just what is pleasant and to be desired. You are to give thanks in every hard, difficult situation in life.

In everything, find something to be thankful for. Be thankful you have a God who commands you to give thanks and shift your attention away from the things of this world. Be thankful that God is good. Be thankful that God is stronger than all else combined. Be thankful that God loves the whole world. Be thankful that God is kind, not just to the righteous, but also to the unthankful and the unholy. Be thankful that God sends rain on the just and on the unjust. Be thankful that you can trust Him to do what is best for all concerned. Be thankful that He is God and that He is in control.

Be thankful that you are saved and Jesus is coming again to receive you unto Himself. Be thankful that you are filled with the Holy Spirit. [18] Be thankful that Jesus has given you authority over all the power of the enemy. Don't feel bad because such a little thing is making it hard for you to be thankful. Ask God to help you give thanks. And don't justify your lack of thanksgiving because the problem is so big. God is bigger.

Be thankful for your time. Better is one day in God's courts than thousands elsewhere. Be thankful for your resources. Little is much when God is in it. Be thankful for your abilities. One yielded finger to the Lord is better than a whole body unyielded.

---

18. If you are not, you can pray this prayer: "Lord Jesus, come into my heart and fill me with Your Holy Spirit." You can be sure that He will.

If you can't seem to pray your way out of a situation, then remember Joseph. [19] Joseph escaped destruction, only to end up being sold as a slave. Then he went from being a favored servant to being imprisoned. But, for Joseph, prison was the right place at the right time to save himself, his family, and his whole nation. It became the place to receive God's blessing. Be thankful that God is working on your behalf.

Be thankful that the Lord is your Shepherd. He has come to seek and to save that which was lost. He would leave the ninety and nine, to go in search of that one. He will save to the uttermost. He will save you from all your thoughts and besetting sins. He will save your loved ones. He will save you completely. He will deliver you. He will see you through.

---

16. See Genesis 37 and 39-50.

Chapter

9

Get A Revelation Knowledge of God's Love

Herein is love, not that we loved God, but that he loved us, and sent his Son to be the propitiation [atoning sacrifice] for our sins. [20]

---

20. 1 John 4:10, KJV

For God so loved the world, that he gave his only begotten Son, that whosoever believeth in him should not perish, but have everlasting life. For God sent not his Son into the world to condemn the world; but that the world through him [Jesus] might be saved. [21]

This is love. How much does God love you? He loved you enough to give His only begotten Son for you. Jesus shed His own blood for you. He suffered and bled and died for your life. He tenderly washes you with His own blood, so that you are completely clean. No one else would do that. No one else *could* do that. God has made you clean. What God has cleansed, do not call common.

Receive the truth that God loves you more than anything. He treasures you. You are worth everything to Him. He

21. John 3:16-17, KJV

wants to spend all of eternity with you. He sees all the bad you have ever done, all the things you can't tell anyone, but He will wash it all away with His precious blood. This is the only thing that can cleanse you. Jesus is the only name that can save you. Call upon the name of the Lord and be saved.

Let the truth of God's love permeate your life. You can trust Him. He definitely loves you. He loves those you love and those for whom you are concerned. All that He did for you, He also did for them. He loves them just the same. You can trust the Lord to care for your loved ones. He is worthy of your trust.

Knowing that God loves you is an important step toward your new joy-filled life. This is a secure foundation upon which you can to build. When trials come, rest upon the truth that God is good and that He loves you. You can move forward with God.

Receive this truth by faith or, if needed, ask God to help you know the truth. Then, let the truth of God's love set you free. Know the truth of Jesus Christ. Even if you don't feel like it is true, it still is. The Son of God is shining over you in all His glory. His love never fails. He is ever-faithful. Don't waste your time doubting the truth of God's love.

If doubts or questions do arise, give them over to the Lord, and receive His answers. Come to the point where the first answer you have is: "Jesus loves me. Of this I am sure."

God's truth is your solid rock. It is your firm foundation. You can build your life on the truth of God's love. It is immovable. Solid. Firm. Unchanging. On this foundation, your house will stand.

Chapter
10

Pray the Scriptures

Pray the Scriptures. The Word of God is your sword in the Spirit. It is powerful and effective. It will accomplish all that God intends. His Word cannot return to Him empty.

Pray the Scriptures over your family, your loved ones, your friends, your church, and yourself. Pray the Scriptures in every situation. Let the truth of God's Word be loosed into the lives of your loved ones and into your own. Line up your prayers with the Word of God. Let His Kingdom come and His will be done. Let it be on earth, as it is in Heaven.

The sword of the Spirit is your offensive weapon. It is quite effective when dealing with enemy attacks. When Jesus was tempted in the wilderness, He responded with, "It is written." Jesus, the example we are to follow, used scripture to combat the enemy. Jesus, the living Word of God, allowed the written Word of God to be His defense. How much more do we need to pray the words of God over our lives?

God's Word will be a lamp unto your feet and a light unto your path. It will show you any needed course corrections for your life and your prayers. Scriptural prayers will help you get in agreement with God. They will help you get the attitude you need.

Scriptural prayers put your focus on the Lord. They take your thoughts captive and make them obedient to Christ. Scriptural prayers will lead you into prayers of thanksgiving and worship and faith. Scriptural prayers will help you wait on the Lord and renew your strength. Scriptural prayers will let you draw water from the wells of salvation with joy. Scriptural prayers will lead you on in the paths of life.

Praying the Word of God reinforces its truths in your life. Pray God's prayers out loud. Let them be loosed into the atmosphere. Let them go out like seed. Water them with more prayers. Then, get ready for a bountiful harvest.

When you do this, you are not trying to force your will on God. Instead, you are saying, "Your kingdom come. Your will be done." Praying the Scriptures is surrendering to God's will and His way. God's ways are best. Get on the path of life.

Chapter
11

Don't Give Up

For you have need of endurance, so that after you have done the will of God, you may receive the promise.[22]

Endurance is very important to your success. You may not see results immediately. If you do, then *hallelujah*! But if not, you will need to keep going until

---

22. Hebrews 10:36

you break through into the presence of God. In His presence is fullness of joy. In His presence is rest. You will eventually break through — if you do not give up. God is faithful to keep His promises. He is not slack, or forgetful, or disorganized. Stay disciplined to keep doing the right things, the things God has commanded you to do. You will see results.

Don't give up just before the finish line. Know the truth, and let the truth set you free. Take the last step, as well as the first. Make sure you enter the Promised Land. *"God is not asking you to do what you cannot do."* [23] He will make a way in the wilderness and give you rivers in the desert. You are His people, His chosen. He has chosen you to proclaim His praise.

Discipline is not always easy, even when we know firsthand the rewards

23. Jon Webster, Children's Pastor at Evangel Worship Center, Concord, North Carolina

of obedience. Ask God to be at work within you, both to will, and to do, of His good pleasure. Let God be the Author and the Finisher and the Perfecter of your faith.

If you slip up, and suddenly your life is not so joyful, begin again with God. He is the Author of new beginnings. His mercies are new every morning. We are called to bless those who curse us, to pray for those who despitefully use us and persecute us. We are to be kind, even to the unthankful and unholy. As we respond in this way and commit the outcome to the Lord, we have the peace of God. Because we have chosen His way, the rest is now His business. Don't give up. Receive your promise.

Don't stop, whatever the circumstance. Keep doing the disciplines because you know they are the right thing to do. Reading the Word of God, keeping your thoughts captive, prayer, and praise and worship are daily necessities for a healthy, happy, joy-filled life. Let these disciplines be a daily part of your new joy-filled life. You are pleasing God. Keep your eyes on Jesus. He is always good. He is always worthy to be praised.

Praise is your vehicle out of the wilderness. Don't stop praising until you get out. Then praise Him because you are out. Enter His courts with praise. Come before His presence with singing. Come before the King of kings. He will not deny you any good thing. He loves you. He is so good.

Worship God. Give Him the glory. He is worthy.

God is greater than you or your circumstances. Let Him have His way. Let Him have all the glory, honor, and praise.

Chapter
12

The Blood of Jesus Is There for You

The blood of Jesus Christ ... cleanses us from all sin. [24]

The blood of Jesus cleanses you from all sin. You might say, "You don't know what happened." It doesn't matter. The truth is still the truth. The Word of God

24. 1 John 1:7

says that the blood of Jesus cleanses you from all sin. All. Not just the sins you have committed, but also the sins that have been committed against you. Every sin, large or small, overwhelmingly great, or far too miniscule to mention, they are all gone.

"Don't let the enemy lie to you, saying, "You have this issue, or there is this issue in your family."[25] Lighten your load. Let go of the past. Your past is under the blood of Jesus. No one can change what has happened, but you can change. You can be who God wants you to be. You can be anything He says you can be. You can do anything He says you can do. You have a future with God.

The truth is that you are clean. The devil can lie and say you are not clean, but the devil is a liar. He can hold up an ugly picture and say, "That is you,"

25. Brenda Naska, missionary to the Philippines with FIRE International

but that is not you. You are being conformed to the image of Jesus Christ. Our Savior is spotless, sinless, beautiful to behold.

The Word of God is our mirror. We are what God says we are in His Word. The Bible says we are cleansed and beautiful. We are vessels of honor. Dressed in our garments of praise, crowned with His lovingkindness, armed with the Sword of the Spirit, we worship our God in spirit and in truth.

Joy gives us the strength to dress ourselves in the beautiful garments He provides. Joy gives us strength to pick up our sword and defend ourselves against the wiles of the enemy. Joy gives us endurance to run with patience the race laid out before us. We are lovely, glorious, made in His image.

The past is gone, obliterated, wiped out. Written in the sand, it has been washed away by an ocean of God's love. Praise the Lord. We are overcomers. The past is not who we are. Don't worry about what other people are thinking about you. *And don't let past hurts, past failures, or old ways of thinking hold you back.* [26] The past is not you. Step out into your future with God!

---

26. I learned this truth from Joe McManus, Worship Leader, Evangel Worship Center, Concord, North Carolina.

Chapter
13

Give It to the Lord

There are some things that are too big, too hard, or too awful for us to handle. Nothing we can say or do will alter or change them. They are so horrendous we cannot explain them. Give these things to the Lord. These are things that we really can't deal with, so don't even try. Let the Lord handle them.

If others persist in asking, "Why?," refer them to the Lord. Then move on to thinking on something good, pure, or lovely. Think on a good report. Think on something with virtue or praise.

Your job is to follow Jesus. Look to Him. Obey His instructions one step at a time. Let Him deal with the world and all its problems. He is bigger than all your problems. He is bigger than any situation. Always remember: great big God, little bitty problem. He's big enough to take care of this situation. He's big enough to take care of you. He's big enough to take care of all your loved ones. He will bring you through.

Cast your burden on the LORD, and He shall sustain you. [27]

---

27. Psalm 55:22

Chapter
14

Know the
Importance of Joy

Herein is my Father glorified, that ye bear much fruit. [28]

The fruit of the Spirit is ... joy. [29]

In Isaiah 65:13-14, a contrast is shown between those who serve God and those

---

28. John 15:8, KJV
29. Galatians 5:22, KJV

who do not. God's servants shall eat and drink. They are not hungry or thirsty. God's servants shall rejoice. God's servants shall sing for joy of heart. Joy and rejoicing are a sign of the Lord's possession. You belong to Him. Your joy is a sign to others that you belong to the Lord Jesus Christ.

Righteousness by faith in Christ is linked with joy and praise. You are to greatly rejoice in the Lord. Your soul is to be joyful in God. You can rejoice because He has clothed you in garments of salvation. He has covered you in a robe of righteousness. Everlasting joy is yours. Mourning is removed and replaced by joy. Depression is replaced by praise. Go through the gates of praise, and enter everlasting joy. Let your days of mourning be ended, for God has commanded you to rejoice.

Consider Jesus, who, for the joy set before Him, endured the cross. How could anyone willingly endure the cross? Yet for the joy set before Him, Jesus did. It was the joy of your salvation, the joy of bringing many sons to glory.

How can you bear your cross? Through the joy of your salvation. How can you endure? Through the power of God. He is so good. He will help you.

Joy is not selfish. It trusts that God loves you and will bring all good things. Joy will help others out of despair. If you can see light and hope, then they can too. First they see it in you, and then they can begin to believe for themselves. They begin to hope and look for God's answer.

God's joy is contagious. The time spent waiting on Him is no longer spent in despair. The time spent waiting becomes a joyous time, as you expectantly look for God to move. In your soul, there is joyous anticipation of God's expected end, a future, and a hope.

The joy in your life will cause faith to spring forth in the lives of others, faith to receive their miracle. For many, joy itself will be a miracle. Others may say, "You should be miserable." But God says you can have life, joy, and peace. You can have the joy of the Lord for your strength to overcome.

In Isaiah we read,

And in that day you will say:

"O Lord, I will praise You;
Though You were angry with me,
Your anger is turned away, and You comfort me.
Behold, God is my salvation,
I will trust and not be afraid;

'For Yah, the LORD, is my strength and song;
He also has become my salvation.' "

Therefore with joy you will draw water
From the wells of salvation.[30]

Let us become so filled with the Spirit of God that whatever happens, our response will be to praise God. He will still be God. He will still be good. No matter how bad the situation, our God is in control. He will have His way. Praise God for what He is doing, not what the enemy is trying to do. Remember the cross.

God is in charge. If you can't see any good, look to the Lord and praise Him by faith. Trust in Him, and He will bring it to pass. Do it as an act of the will, by faith, in humble reliance on the Holy Spirit.

---

30. Isaiah 12:1-3

Speak out God's truth. Praise Him that your afflictions are only light and momentary. Praise Him that they are working for you an eternal weight of glory. Every day is one step closer to the revealing of God's glorious divine expected end. Thank God in advance for His answer. Then get ready to enjoy it.

Believe the truth. Get ready for His Blessing. Be joyful in hope. Expectantly look for His coming. Don't waste your time believing the lies of the enemy. Put your faith and confidence in the Lord. He is able to do what He has promised. He is able to do exceeding abundantly above all you can ask or think. His arm is not shortened that it cannot save. His ear is not hardened that He cannot hear.

Rejoice in the Lord!

Chapter
15

Count It All Joy

My brethren, count it all joy when you fall into various trials, knowing that the testing of your faith produces patience.[31]

We glory in tribulations also: knowing that tribulation worketh patience, and patience, experience; and experience, hope.[32]

---

31. James 1:2-3
32. Romans 5:3-4, KJV

When we are going through a very tough time, we are instructed to *"count it all joy."* You are to know that this is merely a testing of your faith. Your faith is genuine, and this trial will show you just what kind of faith you have. Fully, completely, totally rely on God to supply all your needs. You cannot lose. Be secure in the fact that God loves you and your loved ones. Trust in the work that Jesus Christ did on the cross for your salvation. Look to Him to provide your righteousness. Find your answers in the Lord. Begin to move forward in your life with God.

God knows the answers already. Your trials are not for His benefit; they are for yours. God wants you to know for sure that you are saved. He wants you to know for sure the great depths of His love. He wants you to lack no good thing. This testing produces patience, and patience will have a perfect work in your life. It is to make you complete, that you may lack nothing.

Rejoice in the fact that all things work together for good to them that love God. You are called according to His purpose. You are predestined to be conformed to the image of God's Son. God has called you. God has justified you. God is for you. Nothing and no one can stand against you. Nothing is able to separate you from the love of God that is yours in Christ Jesus our Lord. Don't waste time believing the lies of the enemy. Rejoice in the Lord your God. Know the truth.

God does not want you to be miserable, so do not accept misery. In your trials, rejoice in the Lord. Know the truth. Be free in Christ Jesus to rejoice in every situation. Count it all joy. Just as the cross became Jesus' greatest victory, so you can turn every trial into triumph. Let every moment be a moment of thanksgiving, a time of joy.

Faith Brings Joy

Therefore, since we have been made right in God's sight by faith, we have peace with God because of what Jesus Christ our Lord has done for us. Because of our faith, Christ has brought us into this place of undeserved privilege where we now stand, and we confidently and joyfully look forward to sharing God's glory.

We can rejoice, too, when we run into problems and trials, for we know that they help us develop endurance. And endurance develops strength of character, and character strengthens our confident hope of salvation. And this hope will not lead to disappointment. For we know how dearly God loves us, because he has given us the Holy Spirit to fill our hearts with his love.

When we were utterly helpless, Christ came at just the right time and died for us sinners. Now, most people would not be willing to die for an upright person, though someone might perhaps be willing to die for a person who is especially good. But God showed his great love for us by sending Christ to die for us while we were still sinners. And since we have been made right in God's sight by the blood of Christ, he will certainly save us from God's condemnation. For since our friendship with God was restored by the death of his Son while we were still his enemies, we will certainly be saved through the life of his Son. So now we can rejoice in our wonderful new relationship with God because our Lord Jesus Christ has made us friends of God. [33]

---

33. Romans 5:1-11, NLT (given to me by Crystal Hudson through a wonderful sister in the Lord at CMC University Hospital, Charlotte, North Carolina)

Acknowledgements

First of all, I would like to acknowledge the Lord Jesus Christ. He gave me this book. And when I needed to read it, He had me write it. Many others could have written the book, but I am thankful to have had the privilege of writing it.

I would also like to acknowledge all the members of the Body of Christ who would let me know by a word or comment that it was time to write the book or that it was time to begin working on a specific chapter. They never knew, but I always did.

I specifically want to thank Ann Pope for her poems and Penny Webster for her editorial help. I would also like to thank Crystal Hudson for her scriptures.

Finally, thank you to Pastor Thant McManus, Brother Joe McManus, and Brother Jon Webster.

A Prophetic Word by Brenda Naska

You are an army of God. No more chains are holding you back. Don't let the enemy lie to you and tell you,"No, you can't do it. You have this issue, ... you have this issue in your family, you have this issue in yourself." That's not true. The Word of God says you are free. Whoever God sets free is free indeed. I want to call the army to rise up, right now, in Jesus' name. I declare the name of Jesus over you. Rise up, army of God! Rise up in Jesus' name.

Wake up! The Son is shining over you. There is power in the name of Jesus. Don't ever let the enemy lie to you, saying that the name of Jesus is nothing. You can always call on Jesus when your back is on the wall. There is always Jesus. I declare Jesus over you. I declare

Jesus over your life. I declare Jesus over your situations right now.
Wake up! There is a call on you. There is a call for you. Wake up! [34]

---

34. Brenda Naska is a missionary to the Philippines serving with FIRE International.

Notes: